WHO ROLLED THE STONE?

MEDITATIONS & POEMS
ON THE RESURRECTED LIFE

JOYCE CARR
STEDELBAUER

TATE PUBLISHING, LLC

"Who Rolled the Stone?" by Joyce Carr Stedelbauer

Published in the United States of America
by Tate Publishing, LLC
127 East Trade Center Terrace
Mustang, OK 73064
(888) 361–9473

Scripture quotations used in the book were taken from:
Holy Bible, New International Version ®, Copyright © 1973, 1978, 1984 by International Bible Society. Used by permission of Zondervan Publishing House. All rights reserved.
New American Standard Bible ®, Copyright © 1960, 1962, 1963, 1968, 1971, 1972, 1973, 1975, 1977, 1995 by The Lockman Foundation. Used by permission. All rights reserved.
The Living Bible / Kenneth N. Taylor: Tyndale House, © Copyright 1997, 1971 by Tyndale House Publishers, Inc. Used by permission. All rights reserved.
The Message, Copyright © 1993, 1994, 1995, 1996, 2000, 2001, 2002. Used by permission of NavPress Publishing Group.

ISBN: 1-5988642-7-0

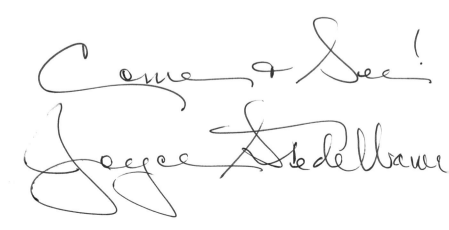

Who Rolled the Stone? was first dramatized
on Coastline Radio, Nerja, Malaga, Spain, for
Easter, 2005. It was created by Michael Chitty
from the book published by Tate Publishing.

DEDICATION

With love and appreciation

to the **W**OMEN **O**F THE **W**ORD

WOW!

Dear friends who walk the green paths
and climb the rocky hills
of the Holy Scriptures with me.

MONDAY MORNING MANNA

Sisters of the heart who steady me
when I stumble and link arms
for the joyous journey.

And always

My George

ACKNOWLEDGEMENTS

Every dark place needs light. Like a tomb,
unless there is a light source nothing can be seen.
Tate Publishing has shone a clear light onto
these pages peopled with those who were the
first to know of the Resurrection.

I appreciate the skilled staff.
They have an admirable dedication to do
excellent work and honor the Lord.

Editor Curtis Winkle
Art Design Sommer Buss
Layout Melanie Harr-Hughes

CONTENTS

STONE

WHO ROLLED THE STONE? COME AND SEE!

FOREWORD

The scriptures teach us that God created man in His own image. How do we find this reality manifested? This book helps answer that question for me. The power of these beautifully crafted words to create new light reveals the image of God at work through one person, Joyce Carr Stedelbauer.

Our God-given ability to create and destroy with our words is often abused. How uplifting it is to read these skillfully crafted words, to discover new light shining creatively on the resurrection and to hear from them new canticles being sung by the characters involved in our Lord's life, death and resurrection. The Imago Dei, the image of God, is at work through Joyce. She has graciously yielded her time and talents to Him for this treasure of new images and new sounds circling the glorious fact that His tomb is empty. The reader will find that her words freshly paint the timeless image of that empty tomb on the canvas of our souls. "He is not dead. He is alive," the angel announced when the women visited the tomb that Easter morning. How fortunate we are to be the recipients of that living hope. How fortunate we are to hear new words convey that truth through the work of my dear friend, Joyce Carr Stedelbauer.

Rev. William Warrick
Senior Pastor
Williamsburg Community Chapel

Everybody dies in Adam;
everybody comes alive in Christ.
I Corinthians 15

WHO ROLLED THE STONE?

MOUNTAINS! BOULDERS! ROCKS! STONES!

*W*e have all stumbled somewhere along a pebbled path. Your way may have led between serrated mountain peaks or through deep blue canyons, breaking out occasionally to a high green plain only to plunge again down a scrabbly slide, grasping at roots for a hand hold. The highway of life is not smooth and easy traveling even though it is paved with good intentions. For then we would never know the need of a pat on the back—an arm around the waist—a leg up—a shoulder to lean on—or a helping hand. We would not need anyone—much less God.

Geologists report myriads of kinds of rock laid down over eons on this shifting planet. But there is only one STONE that really matters—a singular STONE—a solitary STONE that affected the entire world.

Somewhere outside the small, stone-walled city of Jerusalem three crosses scarred the afternoon sky one particular Passover weekend almost 2000 years ago. It was nothing unusual to see Roman crosses of shame in this poor, occupied land. But the central cross split the centuries dividing time before Christ, B. C., and time after He invaded human history, a.d. (Anno Domini) Year of our Lord.

No record remains of the graves for the two thieves crucified on either side of this Man from Nazareth. But His lacerated body was tenderly removed from the crude cross by Nicodemus and Joseph of Arimathea who had boldly gone before Pontus Pilate, the Roman Procurator, and asked for the body of Jesus. Hastily they returned to the infamous hillside as soon the sun would set on this ghastly sight and the body had to be laid to rest before nightfall of Sabbath.

A strange light had returned after the sudden darkness and a horrendous earthquake had rattled the rocks. Men were in shock and fear for the enormous veil in the Temple that separated the Sanctuary from the Holy of Holies had been ripped open from top to bottom to reveal the golden angels guarding the Mercy Seat of the Holy God!

A long white cloth was wrapped around His limp body and under the lifeless arms that once had welcomed little children. The men strained under the weight of His young form, carried Him to Joseph's own unused tomb nearby and gently laid Him on the rocky ledge. Carefully they wrapped His bloody head in His *tallit*—the prayer shawl He had worn and honored since He was recognized as a Man. Tradition states that the sacred shawl may very well have been made by the women in His family from the swaddling clothes that wrapped Him in Bethlehem in His Mother's arms.

Christmas is over. The Star no longer shines over

Bethlehem. The sheep are scattered by shellfire. The Shepherds have moved to the city and gone to Agricultural School. The Wise Men have traveled to Wall Street. The Inn is franchised. The Angel Choir has vaporized and the Choral Guilds have stored the music for the Hallelujah Chorus and Away in A Manger. The last strains have died in the cacophony of New Year's traffic.

What did it all mean? Churches working overtime—family celebrations for the fortunate—a bump in business—the "Make or Break" season—relief for the disenfranchised—the lonely—relief that all the fuss is finished.

But the story has just begun—the ageless story of why a baby born in Bethlehem 2000 + years ago to an obscure family is still a front page story and worthy of CNN headline news. The Passion of the Christ awakened movie goers to a horrific glimpse of the One.

*Keep your eyes on Jesus, who both began
and finished this race we are in. Hebrews 12*

From the cradle to the cross we are fascinated with His Story. How could the death of a humble carpenter so long ago affect my life and offer me any hope of forgiveness for my sin today? In fact, how do I even know that I need to be forgiven? Who says so?

*God sacrificed Jesus on the altar of the world to clear
that world of sin. Having faith in him sets us in the clear.
Romans 3*

This is how much God loved the world: He gave his son,
his one and only son. John 3

We puzzle over the gaps in the Bible, such as Jesus' life from the age of 12 to 30, inventing scenarios to augment His humanity and deity. But when God in the flesh died that awful day, outside the walls of Jerusalem—like a common scapegoat—the rocking world was plunged into pervasive darkness. For He had declared:

I am the world's Light. John 8

She wrapped him in a blanket and laid him in a manger.
Luke 2

Taking him down, he wrapped him in a linen shroud and
placed him in a tomb chiseled into the rock.
Luke 23

All hope was buried in a borrowed tomb. The STONE was rolled into place with a heavy thud. A seal was stamped to the STONE. Temple soldiers were posted to guard the tomb for fear of His disciples stealing away His body for they remembered His words:

After three days I will be raised. Matthew 27

Tear down this Temple and in three days I
will put it back together again. John 2

The STONE of the tomb of Jesus Christ. How would you develop an acrostic on the tombstone of His grave? I am always grateful for the teachers who taught me to think in terms of an acrostic. It helps me to concentrate and focus my meditation.

S IS FOR SAVIOR
T
O
N
E

*A Savior has just been born in David's town,
a Savior who is Messiah and Master. Luke 2*

*We've heard it for ourselves and know it for sure.
He's the Savior of the world. John 4*

*And we have seen for ourselves and continue to state
openly that the Father sent his son to be the Savior of the
world. 1 John 4*

Consistently throughout Scripture, Christ is equated as the Savior for all mankind, all who will believe on His all powerful Name to save them from their sin. John the Baptizer was the first who declared:

*Here He is! God's Passover Lamb!
He forgives the sins of the world. John 1*

*Whoever did want him . . . He made to be their true selves,
their child-of-God selves. John 1*

We are certainly all born as the creation of God but Scripture makes clear that it is our active belief that transforms us into God's children as we come to understand His great gift of grace.

SAVIOR
TOMB
O
N
E

You are like manicured grave plots . . . Matthew 23

Jesus used the place of the dead as a derogatory statement to the faithless. The guilt of the whole world is compared to an open TOMB.

Their throats are gaping graves,
their tongues slick as mud slides. Romans 3

Christ demonstrated His power over death in several miraculous ways before the climactic day of His own resurrection. He had declared that:

I am, right now, Resurrection and Life. John 11

He gave the Widow of Nain back her son alive when he was already in his coffin. He told Jarius to return home and he would find his little girl alive, even though the servant had pronounced her dead. And after His friend had been four days in the TOMB, Jesus called in a loud voice:

Lazarus, come out! John 11

*What came into existence was Life,
and that Life was Light to live by. John 1*

*It's urgent that you listen carefully to this, anyone here
who believes what I am saying right now and aligns
himself with the Father . . . has at this very moment the
real, lasting life . . . John 5*

A thinking man will ask who is this John whose words form so much of the Bible, the living Scripture? John was the closest friend of Jesus, His contemporary, an eye witness of most of the events in His life. After His death and resurrection John saw Him, ate with Him, talked with Him, and watched Him return to heaven. Jesus came from Heaven to Bethlehem and He returned to Heaven until He comes again to bring lasting peace to our war-ravaged world.

Of course this is not the John who baptized Jesus. He was martyred as a young man in the court of Herod. This John lived to be the oldest of the disciples, was finally imprisoned for constantly declaring the Good News about Jesus and was exiled under the Emperor Domitian to the island of Patmos in the Aegean sea. There he bowed his head to the amazing vision of the Resurrected Christ in the Revelation and recorded it for all time.

SAVIOR
TOMB
OPEN
N
E

Then I saw Heaven OPEN wide . . . Revelation 19

God OPENS doors to all his goodness. Psalm 34

OPEN my eyes so I can see . . . Psalm 119

OPEN! One of the most welcome words in any language. It's OPEN!

I have OPENED a door for you
that no one can slam shut. Revelation 3

Yes the TOMB is OPEN for all mankind to COME AND SEE!

We also have a door of our heart to which we hold the latch string. Jesus promised:

Look at me. I stand at the door. I knock. If you hear me
knock and OPEN the door, I will come right in and have
supper with you. Revelation 3

Blind eyes shall be OPENED. Isaiah 35

And He went on to OPEN their understanding
of the Word of God. Luke 24

One of my most frequent prayers is for my eyes and understanding to be OPEN to the Scripture that I am reading so that I will not be imprisoned by old ideas that may not be true.

The jailhouse tottered, every door flew OPEN...
Acts 16

Paul and Silas were set free by an Angel after they had been imprisoned and chained for telling the wondrous news of the Resurrected Christ.

Stephen, the first Christian martyr, cried out as he was being stoned:

Oh! I see heaven wide OPEN and the Son of Man
standing at the Father's side. Acts 7

Apparently Jesus stood up to receive Stephen into Glory as we are told that the Resurrected Christ is seated at the right hand of the Father. *Hebrews 1*

SAVIOR
TOMB
OPEN
NOW
E

NOW is the right time to listen, the day to be helped. 11 Corinthians 6

Be up and awake to what God is doing! Romans 13

Salvation comes no other way; no other name has been or will be given to us by which we can we saved, only this one. Acts 4

NOW that Christ has carried our sin on His back to the Cross,

NOW that the debt is paid in full for man's redemption by the sinless Jesus,

NOW that the Tomb is open,

NOW that the veil of the Temple no longer hides God's mercy,

NOW that the Resurrection has been witnessed by over 500 people,

NOW that the disciples have seen Him caught up to Heaven in a cloud,

NOW that countless martyrs have died to get the message

through to us,
NOW is our opportunity to believe.

*Every person who believes that Jesus is, in fact,
the Messiah is God-begotten. 1 John 5*

The world is more fragile than we can fathom. When recent Tsunami waves were triggered by a 9.0 earthquake in the Indian Ocean, the seismograph underneath Central Park in New York registered the rolling action. As we whirl furiously on our tilted axis, what power holds us together and keeps us from vaporizing off into space and into the black holes in the heavens?

*He was there before any of it came into existence
and holds it all together right up to this very moment.
Colossians 1*

SAVIOR
TOMB
OPEN
NOW
ETERNITY

The ancient God is home on a foundation of everlasting arms. Deuteronomy 33

I have it all planned out, plans to take care of you, not abandon you, plans to give you the future you hope for. Jeremiah 29

Teacher, what do I need to do to get ETERNAL LIFE? LUKE 10

The timeless questions for all of ETERNITY have always been, "How do I look at the future? What can I do to plan for that which seems so uncertain? Is forever really forever, or is it an endless cycle of seasons and unrecognizable forms of life? Or is this really all there is, make the best of it, and hope that if there is a God He will remember you kindly? After all, we have tried our best, haven't we? If the only real message to us is to love our neighbor then why did He have to die? He could not really have been God, could He? Just a good but unfortunate teacher, like so many others, and if He could not save Himself from that hideous day then how could He even think of being anyone's SAV-IOR?"

C.S. Lewis has given us the most conclusive logic in his book, *Mere Christianity*, now a classic for fifty years. In it he explains that Jesus has left us only three ways to consider His life. He is either Liar, Lunatic or Lord. If He knew He was not really God, then He lied when He claimed:

The Father who sent me, confirmed me. John 5

I and the Father are one heart and mind. John 10

To see me is to see the Father. John 14

Or if He sincerely believed all of the things He said, was He a lunatic?

I AM the Road, also the Truth, also the Life. John 14

I AM the bread of life. John 6

*Everyone who lives believing in me
does not ultimately die at all. . John 11*

*There is plenty of room for you in my Father's home.
If that weren't so, would I have told you that I'm on my
way to get a room ready for you? John 14*

The only other choice is that He is the Lord of life and ETERNITY.

What is the rest of that story after the disciples fled to huddle in dark homes around a single oil lamp for fear of the authorities? We know a few women dared to return on the morning after the close of Sabbath to anoint the beloved body of their Lord. But few would listen to their breathless news. We know that the Roman soldiers who were posted to guard the Tomb had to report their excuses to their officers and face the punishment of such a serious failing to carry out their orders.

We can be sure that the morning news at the city gates was rampant with rumors:

CRIMINAL ESCAPES TOMB!
THE SWOON THEORY!
BODY STOLEN BY THE DISCIPLES!
HALLUCINATIONS OF ANGELS!
DELIRIOUS WOMEN!
WHO ROLLED THE STONE?

The Angel asked the women:

Why are you looking for the Living One in a cemetery?
Luke 24

In Israel today it is possible to worship in the green garden on the rocky hillside just outside of the Damascus gate or in the cave-like, candlelit interior of the Church of the Holy Sepulcher, which was also outside the city wall at the time of the Crucifixion that changed History. No one can say with certainty the exact location of that Holy Tomb but Matthew reports in his gospel:

After the Sabbath, as the first light of the new week dawned . . . suddenly the earth reeled and rocked under their feet as God's angel came down from heaven . . . he rolled back the STONE and then sat on it. Matthew 28

The STONE was rolled away supernaturally by the Angel of the Lord of Life not just to let Him out but to let the world in to COME AND SEE!

God will do what it takes—whatever it takes
to bring his children home.

Max Lucado

SAVIOR

*The STONE the masons discarded as flawed
is now the capstone! Psalm 118*

*Watch closely, I'm laying a foundation in Zion . . . and this
is the meaning of the Stone: a trusting life won't topple.
Isaiah 28*

*But, our citizenship is in heaven. And we eagerly await
a Savior from there, the Lord Jesus Christ, who by the
power that enables him to bring everything under His
control, will transform our lowly bodies
so that they will be like his glorious body.
Philippians 3*

*Everybody dies in Adam everybody comes alive in Christ.
I Corinthians 15*

Jesus Christ is the tried and true CORNERSTONE of our faith and hope.

It is never blind faith but faith in the Resurrected Christ.

He is the one and only SAVIOR for the world.

ADAM

The Word was first, the Word present to God, God present to the Word. The Word was God, in readiness for God from day one. Everything was created through him; nothing, not one thing—came into being without him. What came into being was life and the life was the Light to live by. John 1

Hope first rose in the heart of Adam when God called him.

"Where are you?" Genesis 3

God gave him a garden home in Eden.

When God began creating the heavens and the earth, the earth was a shapeless, chaotic mass, with the Spirit of God brooding over the dark vapors.
Genesis 1

Then God said: Let us make a man—someone like ourselves to be the master of all life upon the earth and in the skies and in the seas. So God made man like his Maker. Like God did God make man. Man and maid did He make them. And God blessed them. Genesis 1

Where are you Adam?
Jogging mist-draped paths past the leopard's
lair, pausing to pet the tiger's kittens,
admiring the serpent's enameled copper
coat against the coolness of dawn,
an exaltation of larks, sun-silhouetted,
answer the lush cry of wild parrots
unfurling purpled blooms and orange
breeze in the emerald sanctuary.
Music of the planets sings in God-shaped ears.

Where are you Adam?
Husbanding autumnal vines—weighted
amethyst cascades of moon-drops—
plucking figs exploding sweetness on
the tongue like shooting stars—
ducking under jeweled olive branches,
newly ripe as afternoon.
Mother giraffe proudly shows her
somnolent newborn on stilted sticks.
Gazelles halt in mid-flight, marabou
storks, elands and emus crowd
the acacia clearing, monkeys chatter in thorn trees—even
the indifferent ostrich stares in wonder.
Lions and lambs laze watching rhinos
and wart hogs jostle horns, elephants cheer,
while zebras gossip with secretary birds.

Where are you Adam?
Reclining in secure shade of the Tree
of Life, waiting for what
you do not know you need, an elegant
emptiness secreted in your soul.
Searching the lambent sky for that
which you cannot see, listening
for music not yet imagined, breathing
honeyed fragrance not yet tasted,
fingering the softness of silence—dreamless
longing for what has never been.

The Triune Presence speaks—
the Creator's touch is like cool fire—
the Spirit breathes life into Woman.

Genesis 1

LUCIFER

For we are not fighting against people made of flesh and blood, but against persons without bodies—the evil rulers of the unseen world.
Ephesians 6

Lucifer is the name of the angel created by God who rebelled against God. Isaiah describes it most clearly for we who are earthbound:

How you are fallen from Heaven, O Lucifer, son of the morning! How you are cut down to the ground—for you said to yourself—"I will ascend to Heaven and rule the angels. I will take the highest throne. I will climb to the highest Heavens and be like the Most High." Isaiah 14

Pride even penetrated the Garden. Whatever the time in Eden—whether glorious day or star-spangled night—it was the right time. Never early or late, rushed or slow. Roses always bloomed, grass was always a green carpet, animals always played together, fruit was always ripe. An elegant serpent watched the woman from the shade of the Tree of the Knowledge of Good and Evil. He always knew when to find her alone.

Angel of Light—brilliant beauty—created by God,
how is it that you looked into the mirrored dome of heaven
and imagined greater grace?
What august ambition thundered in your being
that you craved position beyond peace?
What greed surfeited your ego that
schemed for selfish power?

Angel of Light to Devil of Darkness,
how fast your fall—laser lightning—
sundering your welcome in the halls of Heaven.
Condemned to relentlessly roam the
crowded corridors of polluted air,
rubbing shoulders with ordinary human beings.

Devil—your very name holds evil—
demented demons your companions, clawing at your heels,
gnawing your very bones—wily as wolves circling a camp
until the appointed day when you move to the pit,
the anteroom of hell—always burning—
never consuming its inmates.

When The Son who crushed you from the Cross
returns to reign forever He will bring the keys
to your eternal cell boiling in the blackness beyond all
Grace, Peace and Power.

Isaiah 14

ABRAHAM

After the gates of Paradise clanged shut, Adam felt the millstone of sin strapped to his back. He could never move freely again. The weight was oppressive. The stone was grinding his flesh. He bent lower every year. Rocks and thistles covered the ground.

God called another man. God had a plan. He gave this man a new land.

Abraham entered into what God was doing for him and that was the turning point. He trusted God to set him right instead of trying to be right on his own. Romans 4

Abraham carried a sharpening stone. Knives were important to a nomadic herdsman in the desert. He always had at least one knife in a leather scabbard on the rope around his waist. His wrists were strong. He could hone a fine edge on his knives. He used rough stones for the initial cuts and progressively smoother stones to polish it so he could split a grain of sand. He had taken particular care with the knife now in his hand.

A resolute man, Abraham, crowned with
age, and the sapling youth, Isaac
faced the forbidding mountain. It stood silent,
with a terrible grace, as if waiting for countless centuries.
Soft sand of the three-day journey
hardened into sun-struck stone;
the sky a relentless blue tent, no trees offering solace,
no breeze to cool a fevered brow.
They shared a deep draught of water
from the goat-skin bag.
He hoisted the firewood onto the boy's back.

Father, where is the lamb? God will provide, my son.

Tears stung his eyes like a scirocco wind, ran down the
grey beard like anointing oil on a priest. Unforgiving rocks
bruised sandaled feet. Air seemed sucked from his lungs.
The peak was as distant as the gates of Heaven.

The resolute Man named Jesus, thorn-
crowned, stumbled against the mountain
of terrible grace. It stood silent, as if
waiting for measured centuries.
The city streets around the mountain
pulsed with people, their shouts
striking like lethal stones on the Man
who spoke of three days hence.
The sky a bruised, blue banner, no
breeze to cool a bloodied brow,

no tree except the one dropped on His beaten back.
Tears of forgiveness ran down His matted beard—
anointing oil on the crucified Priest.

An unlikely mountain to be called *The Joy of the earth,*
not spectacular, snow-covered, or green-
robed with silvery streams,
but a rocky ridge rising from the surrounding valleys.
God proclaimed this same mountain an altar of obedience,
a threshing floor for the winnowing
of grain, a worship site,
a judgment hill, a battlefield, a crossroads
of controversy, and one day,
Mt. Zion, joy of the whole earth.

Psalm 48

JOHN THE BAPTIST

John the Baptist was a man of the land. He used rocks for pulpits to proclaim the astounding message that he was sent to prepare the way for the coming Messiah.

"I am not the Christ . . . I am a voice from the barren wilderness Shouting as Isaiah prophesied, 'Get ready for the coming of the Lord.' . . . Look, there is the Lamb of God who takes away the World's sins. He is the One I was talking about when I said, Soon a Man far greater than I is coming, who existed long before me . . . I didn't know he was the One, but at the time God said when you see the Holy Spirit descending and resting on someone— he is the One you are looking for. He is the One who baptizes with The Holy Spirit. I saw it happen to this Man and I testify that he is the Son of God." John 1

Because of your witness, John,
Catholics and Baptists, Congregationalists
and Presbyterians,
Methodists and all manner of believers baptize
those who follow the Christ.
You were just a man, no ordinary man, a strange man.
A man of the land, dressed in skins,
surviving on locusts and honey, sleeping under the starry
gospel sky or secreted in a cave
when clouds let down their hail of tears.

Prophets promised one like Elijah would precede
the longed for Messiah like winter rains soften the earth.
Dr. Luke chronicled your extraordinary life from Gabriel's
announcement to your untimely death after the dance.

Mary the Virgin attended your mother Elizabeth
through those last laborious months before your
astonished father, the humbled priest, Zacharias,
broke tradition like a common clay cup,
and named you John.

Skeptics and saints call you "The Voice" crying in the
wilderness for repentant sinners to come to the Jordan.
Your pulpit a rock beside a shallow bend in the river.
Sweet water flowed from Mt. Hermon rising in the North,
through the Galilee into the Jordan coursing past Jerusalem
to the Dead Sea where there is no forgiveness.

One diamond morning a window
opened in the ark of Heaven.
A Dove, pure white, graced the burnt-blue sky,
rested on the dripping shoulder of Jesus of Nazareth
as you lifted Him from the baptismal Jordan.
The voice of God thundered in your ears.
Your obedient voice proclaimed,
"The Lamb of God who takes away the sin of the world."

John, you should have received velvet vestments
and a higher pulpit. A bronze likeness could stand
on that river rock; instead your severed head was served
on a silver platter at an obscene orgy
before a common King.

Jesus pronounced your epitaph,
"The finest man born of woman."

The Gospels

THE CRUCIFY CROWD

*The news that Jesus was coming swept through the city
and a huge crowd of Passover visitors took palm branches
and went down the road to meet Him, shouting," The
SAVIOR!"" God bless the King of Israel!" "Hail to God's
Ambassador!" Then the Pharisees said to each other,"
We've lost. Look, the whole world has gone after Him!"
John 12*

How could public opinion sway like those palm trees
in a single week? The storms of self interest and fear lashed
the city with lies and plots until the following week

Pilate asked the people: *"What charges are you
bringing against this man?"*

Angry voices shouted:

*"If he were not a criminal. we would not have handed
him over to you." "Take him yourselves and judge him by
your own law." "But we have no right to execute anyone."
John 18*

Scurrying down the slick labyrinth of rain-dark streets
like rats seeking holes for hiding—
the crucify crowd—
sharp noses twitching with news
of the prisoner taken in the dead of night,
Roman soldiers finally doing something right.

Whiskers working the smell of fresh blood,
beady eyes blinking recognition of fellow black-robed
rodents by their twisting tails of lies.

The money-changers
still smarting at His rebuke,
business scattered like chaff in an angry wind—
crushing losses during this Passover parade.

The hapless farmer
from the Gaderenes, furious
his black-market herd of pigs was dashed to the sea.

The prominent accusers—
forelocks swinging—
clutching jagged stones intended
for the scandalous harlot:

merchants made rich with
light-weighted sacks,

priests offering pious prayer in public,
fingering their knotted fringed shawls,

the beggar's family who existed
on his alms before he walked,

the good Jew who avoided the good Samaritan.

All of these and more—
the doubters, deserters, the proud and powerful
a malevolent current surging
under the narrow arch to Pilate's praetorian.
Their foul breath bruising the air—

"Crucify!"

" Crucify!"

" Crucify!"

John 19

THE JERUSALEM HOUSEWIFE

I have wondered if I had been there, what I would have shouted. Or would I have run away, terrified by the violence erupting in the streets. It was probably necessary to venture out to get a few provisions and, as a woman, I would not have heard all of the accusations and arguments at the city gates. But I feel I would have known He was innocent. I would have heard of His healings, His kindness, His Compassion. Why, He even sat close to the woman's court when He was teaching in the Temple so we, too, could hear. And Oh, His voice! It was strong and silvered, weighted with truth. Pilate, the Roman Governor asked Him:

Are you a King? Then Jesus answered, I was born for that purpose. And I came to bring Truth to the world. All who love the Truth are my followers. What is truth? Pilate exclaimed. John 18

I'm breathless as a deer escaping the hunt—
having just reached the safety of our door.
The crowds have pushed and pummeled me,
carried along in the crush like never before.

No breath of wind bends the trees today.

Sunrise was as still as dew,
red, gold, purple painted banners
like royal robes flung across the blue.

I took only my scarf, basket and a few small coins
to buy the bread and wine, for our family
will gather at sundown for *Seder*,
I will prepare the meal for them happily.
We'll sing and pray for Elijah to come tonight.
We know he must announce The Messiah,
but we know not the day or glorious hour.

Some great, evil uproar charges the city.
Surging—blood-thirsty—vicious yelling—loud
cries demanding that their prisoner be crucified.
O God, I could not speak or breathe in that crowd!
It is but mid-day and I must light the lamp.
What darkness this, that wraps us like a death-shroud?
I fear this day will be long remembered—
Yahweh, have mercy. I wait on my knees, head bowed.

The Gospels

T

TOMB

*And when the crowd that came to see the crucifixion saw
that Jesus was dead they went home in deep sorrow.
As the body was taken away, the women from Galilee
followed and saw it carried into the TOMB. LUKE 23*

A.W. TOZER said, "I leave possessing nothing but faith." He was speaking of his life, but he could also have said such a statement upon seeing the empty TOMB of Christ.

As Mary Magdalene ran to tell Peter:

*They have taken the Lord's body out of the TOMB and I
don't know where they have laid him. Then I went in too,
and saw and believed that he had risen. John 20*

CAIAPHAS

It is a matter of public record that Caiaphas was appointed to the position of High Priest in 18 a.d., an office he held for 18 years including the trial of Jesus.

The High Priest asked him. Are you the Messiah, the Son of God? I Am and you will see me sitting at the right hand of God and returning to earth in the clouds of heaven. Then the High Priest tore his clothes and said, what more do we need? Mark 14

A stone box of bones is mute testimony that Caiaphas lived and died in the early first century. After the flesh had rotted away from a body, the practice was for the relatives to gather the remaining bones and put them in a stone box called an ossuary signed and dated with the name and dates of the deceased. At the dawn of the 21st century just such a box was unearthed in Jerusalem during building excavations. The name was Caiaphas.

Caiaphas, Historians have noted your name.
You lived more than 2 millennia ago,
lived and breathed the Law,
rose to high fame as a priest, following

Annas, your father-in-law.
He sent the celebrated prisoner to you,
now high priest of the land.
How little you knew when you
judged it was expedient that
"One should die for all."

Caiaphas, archeologists have found your box of bones.
A stone ossuary chiseled with proof of your position—
title, name, date—now it stands unlocked.
Mute testimony to the Gospels who mention you,
your palace and cold courtyard.

We read of your now believing servant, Malchus—
his ear healed by the touch of the
Prisoner's shackled hand.
We read of your servant girls, squabbling like hens,
pecking Peter to denial before the rooster crowed again.

Caiaphas, anthropologists have examined your bones.
A box for bones, gathered by some
forgotten, blood-cursed son
after your censorious flesh had rotted away.
No eyes left that once had looked on Him
"who knew no sin"
No evidence of a heart that beat with lawless pride.
No lungs with air to shout condemnation on the Creator.

WHO ROLLED THE STONE?

Caiaphas, you strut briefly on a stage
in passion plays and movies,
lavishly robed in turban and ephod, but on Judgment Day
your box of bones will stand up and bow down
before Him, the Prisoner you condemned.

The Gospels

CAIAPHAS' SERVANT

When Judas betrayed Jesus in the garden on that black night Peter slashed off the right ear of the High Priest's servant. But Jesus said:

Don't resist anymore. And he touched the place where the man's ear had been and restored it. Luke 22

This was the last miracle of Jesus while He was on earth. From changing water into wine at the wedding in Cana to an instant healing in a dark garden the Lord was always concerned for others and their needs.

The slashing off of your ear
                barely stung
so swift was Peter's sword,
                anger in the face of injustice,
yet the healing touch of Jesus
                seared your mind,
cauterized your thinking as you escorted Him
                to the illegal trial.

Only God can heal,
                can give new life.

WHO ROLLED THE STONE?

This man allowed his hands to be bound,
*   his healing hands.*
Could he be the Hosanna of God,
*   the longed for Messiah,*
as the crowd had shouted,
*   waving palms as if a King were coming?*

Your head throbbed like thunder
        as you led him away.
If tears of knowing
        washed your face,
You were the last to be eternally healed before
        the Great Physician's hands were pierced.

I wonder, did Van Gogh ever read of you,
*   long for the Resurrection's healing touch*
when he poured out his
*   blue, blue soul*
into God's starry, starry night?

John 18

PONTIUS PILATE

Herod Agrippa I in a letter to the Emperor Caligula spoke of Pilate "as naturally inflexible, a blend of self-will and relentlessness."

Early in the morning the chief priests, the elders and teachers of religion, the entire Supreme Court, met to discuss their next step, their decision was to send Jesus under armed guard to Pilate, the Roman governor. Pilate asked him: Are you the King of the Jews? Yes, Jesus replied, it is as you say. Then the chief priests accused him of many crimes, and Pilate asked him, why don't you say something? What about all these charges against you? But Jesus said no more. Mark 15

Pilate had a thankless job in Judea, far from the authority and glamour of the Roman Forum where the real decisions were made. His only hope was to keep these rabble-rousing crowds under control and then perhaps he would be recalled to his beloved City on seven hills and given a new white toga. But first he had to deal with this Jesus.

Pilate, what did you do after you condemned Him?
Pools of blood marred the Praetorian stones; water spots
dripped from guilty hands, mute mockery in hours alone.
Soldiers hurried the raucous crowds away, murderous
shouts echoed in a throbbing head. Your wife
nowhere to be seen, since she warned of her dream.

The morning darkened like torturous thoughts.
Black gloom shrouded your soul.
Cursing Caesar for this outpost of fractious Jews,
you paced the halls, passing mirrors winking back
blood-shocked eyes in a haggard face.
Lighted torches needed now at mid-day?
Had the world gone mad? Suddenly—
the earth heaved—groaned—goblets shattered—
rocks split—the floor cracked—was deathly still.

Where is a servant?
Send a message to Herod, (once enemy, now accomplice),
lounging in Tiberius by the inland sea, ask privately,
What did you think of Him?

Perhaps after the Passover Plot, (as some called it),
you fled to Caesarea by the great sea—linking to Rome—
but there was no peace in the palace.
Wind moaned—waves thrashed—crashed
on the rocks below your window and
you were lonely in your bed.

Seeking distraction another day did you hurry to your
reserved seat in the amphitheatre only to see specters stalk
upon that magnificent stage with the sea backdrop?

Today, seeking anonymity, you might escape
to the green links beside the great, blue sea.

But the little white ball still mocks like a mirror,
and your theatre seat is empty in the British Museum's
halls of ancient history.

The Gospels

PILATE'S WIFE

Just then as he was presiding over the court, Pilate's
wife sent him this message: Leave that good Man alone;
for I had a terrible nightmare concerning him last night.
Matthew 27

Fear gripped her with an icy hand on her throat. She could not make her husband listen. She had stayed with him at this posting, far from the social scene of the capital, she had worn last season's gowns, even endured that colossal bore, Herod, when necessary. Actually the estate on the Mediterranean in Caesarea was more than tolerable, but she hated Jerusalem.

What a terrible choice!
Disagreeing with your husband
raising a warning voice
because of a dream.

Not relevant of course,
this is business, it seems.

You needn't have bothered your pretty head
nor worried about what the crowd said.

Though you knew
this trial was all wrong,
condemning in the night
shouting in the throng.

Perhaps you pled with tears one final moment,
spilling all your fears on his Roman robe.

You didn't understand,
his job was on the line.

No time now for remorse,
maybe later, another time . . .
after the lashings, after the Cross,
after the darkness, after the Tomb.

You feared all was lost.

Pilate washed his hands of this,
pronounced no guilt found.

Did he ever recognize his own?

Did you ever dream again?

Matthew 27

THE CENTURION

When the Captain of the Roman military unit handling the
executions saw what had happened, he was stricken with
awe before God and said, surely this man was innocent.
Luke 23

The Centurion was hardened to hideous scenes like this. Crucifixion was the main form of death executed by the Roman government. He saw his distasteful job as a necessary evil in order to be promoted someday and ordered to a Roman legion, perhaps sailing the fresh winds of the Mediterranean.

I serve Caesar.
I am loyal, rigorously trained, stronger than chains
that bind our prisoners and proud to be born Roman.
Not like these poor, pitiful Jews that scurry
about these dusty streets like dogs, whimpering
every time I pass on my powerful horse, as if
I would ever bother with them at all.
I am assigned only to serve Pontus Pilate,
Governor of Judea.

This newest Prisoner must be extremely important—
arrested in the night and already sent to the Praetorian.

Make haste, my steed!
Whoa—Who is this?
Beaten bloody beyond recognition—
like fresh meat dripping at the butcher's stall—
He is a Jew, but why before Pilate?

I slapped His face for impudence—but—
O, His eyes—
Others plucked His beard—I—I could not—
but I spit upon Him in utter contempt.
O—but, His eyes were deep pools of sorrow.
I pressed a royal robe upon His raw shoulders, but
there was no anger in His eyes.

All the tortured way to the place of the skull
He never spoke, groaned yes, but never
complained under the agony of the Cross.
The jeering crowd mocked, cursed and reviled Him.

I choked on the dust, wiped horror from my face,
clutched my raging belly. I held the nails—
the hammer blows struck—one—two—three.
Stumbling aside, I embarrassed myself in the weeds.
He spoke from the Cross—guttural words, piercing words,
of the Father, Thirst, and Forgiveness.
O, His eyes—His eyes locked with mine—

Now, I serve the Crucified Christ.

I am loyal,
rigorously forgiven,
stronger than chains which bound my soul
and humbled to be a follower of this Jew.

Matthew 27

THE TWO THIEVES

When they got to the place called Skull Hill, they crucified
him, along with the criminals, one on his right the other
on his left. One of the criminals hanging alongside him
cursed him : Some Messiah you are! Save Yourself! Save
us! But the other one made him shut up: Have you no fear
of God? You're getting the same as him. We deserve this
but not him . . . Jesus, remember me when You come into
Your Kingdom. He said, don't worry I will. Today you will
join me in Paradise Luke 23

A thief hung on either side,
one lives, the other died.
Both were guilty of their sin.
One Thief cursed,
the other confessed
Him to be the suffering Son of God.

Their scourging was not as brutal.
His blood alone filled the Crucible
of Salvation, paid in full for all
men and women condemned at the Fall.
The repentant are redeemed
by the forgiving Son of God.

A thief hung on either side,
that dreadful day when Love died.

All hope sealed within the Tomb.

Death consumed the world in gloom
until five hundred people saw
the victorious Son of God.

Luke 23

BARABBAS

Pilate called together the chief priests and other Jewish leaders, along with the people and announced his verdict: You have brought this man to me—I have examined him thoroughly and find him innocent. Luke 23 Then Pilate went out again to the people and told them: He is not guilty of any crime. But you have a custom of asking me to release someone from prison each year at Passover. So if you want me to, I will release the 'King of the Jews.' But they screamed back, No, not this man but Barabbas! And he released Barabbas, the man in prison for insurrection and murder. Luke 23

The evidence was overwhelming. The trials, starting in the middle of the night, were illegal by their own law. The witnesses were contradictory. He was betrayed. Nothing was found to be true in the accusations. But the will of the people swayed the mind of Pilate until he turned Jesus over to the voracious crowd and washed his hands, seeking to wash away his own guilt. But what of Barabbas?

Barabbas. where did you go,
suddenly freed from death row?

Cowering under a filthy hood,
hiding in the "crucify" crowd
stood gazing up at Him
who knew no sin.

Did a nail not stab your heart,
understanding He bled your part
of punishment due?

Barabbas, was your mouth not dry
when He thirsted, cried,
"Why"?

Did you not consider your dirty hands,
murderer, prisoner,
when crimson bands of blood
crowned His brow;
offering opportunity to bow?

Yet, He forgave you.

You slipped through the mocking crowd—
a serpent's son—
wrapped your enameled skin in a stinking shroud.

Barabbas, we hear of you no more,
slithering through death's door.

Matthew 27

MARY AT THE CROSS

Every mother has communication beyond the need of words with a son. A soldier's mom will say, "He died doing what he wanted most to do. His purpose was to serve his country." From Gabriel's astonishing commission to Mary, all the way to Jesus' last prayer, you knew. You knew that He was much more than an ordinary, human man. A man about His Father's business, He said. You wisely treasured and pondered all of these things in your heart.

"I am the Way and the Truth and the Life. No one can get to the Father except by means of Me. If you had known who I am, then you would have known who my Father is. From now on you know Him and have seen Him." John 14

"And a sword shall pierce your heart." Luke 2

Mary, the sword of unspeakable pain plunged deeper
within your heart with each agonized breath He drew.
The rapier tip probed tender flesh between rib and breast,
working blade against bone.

"Flesh of my flesh and bone of my bone." Genesis 2

Each cry of His anguish reverberated back
from the cimmerian caverns of your mind.
Straining to comprehend such horrendous cruelty,
you sank to your knees. Prayer for it all to be finished
slipped from silent lips formed to the habit of praise.

Leaning on John you stood carved like two stone pillars
of palpable grief against the blackening sky.

John 19

OPEN

*The next evening when the Sabbath ended, Mary
Magdalene, Salome and Mary the mother of James went
out and purchased embalming spices. Early the following
morning, just at sunrise, they carried them to the TOMB.
On the way they were discussing how they could ever roll
aside the huge STONE from the entrance. But when they
arrived they looked up and saw the STONE—a very heavy
one— was already moved away and the entrance was
OPEN. Mark 15*

The quiet confidence of the women that they could
do something for their Lord is encouraging to women today.
Even though the obstacles seem overwhelming—enormous
stones—beyond our own resources to move them, it is
always right to face the problem. And they went at the first
possible moment just in the pale light of dawn. They could

have knelt at the TOMB and worshipped Him. They could have prayed for wisdom as to what to do now that He was gone. They carried the spices trusting that there would be some way in. To their amazement they found the TOMB OPEN!

THE RESURRECTION ANGEL

For two millennia propositions and proposals have been debated by the most learned minds of the ages. From the "swoon" theory to the "stolen" theory countless attempts have been made to expose the Resurrection of Jesus Christ as anything but true.

But the fact is that the disciples could not have shouldered the weighty STONE that was rolled down a channel and thudded into place over the entryway to the dark recesses. And there was the penalty of death for anyone caught tampering with the seal affixed to the outside of the STONE. Certainly the women could not budge it and they reported it OPEN and empty! Angels were all around. Matthew said there was an earthquake and an Angel came down to roll the Stone and sat on it. Mark mentions one Angel sitting on the right side of the ledge where He lay. Luke reports two Angels standing and John records that Mary Magdalene spoke with two Angels seated where His body had lain. And of course the whipped Man could not have accomplished His own escape. Remember He had stumbled under the weight of the cross and Simon of Cyrene had had to carry it the rest of the sorrowful way to the place of the skull.

WHO ROLLED THE STONE?

Angels splitting the stars
lightning streaks
tracing the moon,
white strobes trailing linen robes

great glistening wings spread in the third heaven

swooped to earth with supersonic speed.
Laser eyes
searched black gloom
for a solitary tomb

somewhere outside the walls of Jerusalem

wing-wind
scattered the sleeping guards.
You shouldered the STONE
grinding the seal to dust,
the earth heaved,
gasped relief,
the garden lay hushed in expectancy.

The Creator stood beside His collapsing burial cloth
slowly releasing the beloved form.
Scarred hands folded the bloody headpiece
laid it separately, alone
and He was
Gone.

Were you one Angel or two
dispatched with haste
from the highest heaven?
Were you seated at the head and
foot of the limp linen cloth
or just one of you near the side where He was pierced?
Or did you wait alone for the frightened disciples
while seated on the impossible STONE?

Skeptics, cynics and rationalists
of the world
have no explanation.
The matchless message
is as clear as Resurrection morning.

He is not here,
He is Risen!

Mark 16

JOSEPH OF ARIMATHEA

A wealthy man. A pious man. A political man, member of the Sanhedrin. His home was in the town of Arimathea in southern Samaria. As a man of high position he dared to approach and request the body of Jesus from Pilate at some risk to himself.

As a devout Jew he would be made unclean by handling a dead body and therefore unable to participate in the Passover to begin that evening. It is Jewish law that a corpse be buried before sundown on the day of death. Victims of Crucifixion were usually left hanging until the vultures cleaned their bones. But Joseph's heart was not for himself but for his Lord. Mark and Luke record:

He was looking for the kingdom of God. Mark 15

Joseph of Arimathea your mellifluous name is as familiar
to Easter Worshippers as the stirring greeting,
He is Risen!

And yet we know you not—
did your good Jewish mother in the village of Arimathea
give you your famous name in honor
of the brave young slave

who became a ruler in Egypt, saving
the nation from starvation?
I doubt she knew of the other Joseph, the
poor carpenter from Nazareth.
You, Joseph became a wealthy member of the Sanhedrin
in Jerusalem—the seventy-one man council—
prominent as the long tassels on your *tallit*.

And yet we know you only briefly—
a secret disciple of Jesus, the man
of no reputation but His own.
You pulled on your beard, till it burned like fire
on your face, puzzling to reconcile
prophecies of the Messiah
on a white horse with this humble
healer on a borrowed ass.
You debated long after the last lamp
was snuffed, with Nicodemus,
another fearful follower of the Teacher from Galilee.

Yet we know your courage defeated fear—
you ran, tassels on your prayer shawl streaming like tears,
stood boldly before Pilate and begged the crucified body.

Nicodemus brought long lengths of linen
to hastily wrap the macerated, bloody flesh.
Together you laid him in your own tomb—
hand hewn—and saw his blood on your skin.

Yet, we do know you, Joseph, as like ourselves—
frightened of the future,
cautious of our reputation,
experiencing burgeoning belief
but digging our own tombs
until we know with confidence,

He is Risen, indeed!

John 19

NICODEMUS

A Pharisee, devout member of the Sanhedrin, Nicodemus is remembered for his late night visit to Jesus. Was he avoiding the crowds that always pressed close to the Teacher? Or did he not want to be observed by the fellow dissenting Jews of his party. Much less by the Sadducees, there was enough disagreement with them. So he came by night to ask his burning question:

"Rabbi, we know that you are a teacher come from God for no one can do these signs that you do, unless God is with him." Jesus replied," with all of the earnestness I possess I tell you this: unless you are born again, you can never get into the Kingdom of God.." "Born again! What do you mean? How can an old man go back into his mother's womb and be born again?" " What I am telling you so earnestly is this: Unless one is born of water and the Spirit, he cannot enter the Kingdom of God. Men can only reproduce human life, but the Holy Spirit gives new life from Heaven." John 3

Nicodemus, I see you in the shadows.
You . . . you who came by night as all seeking sinners do,
out of the dark depths of self—murky motives—wrapped

in a midnight cloak, hiding from pious, fellow Pharisees.
Slipping silently along empty streets, stumbling
on the rocky path across the treacherous Kidron Valley
to the garden, the green olive-sweet garden mountainside.

You watched Him kneeling, draped over a rock,
in anguished conversation with His Father.
Peter, James and John sprawled nearby, asleep.

You had noticed His tenderness toward the sick,
listened to audacious claims of Divinity,
watched Him teaching in the Temple,
and so you came,
burdened with the weightiest question of all humanity.

The pivotal question
on which planet Earth tilts on its axis.
The answer unites man and his Maker eternally.
"You must be born again."

Nicodemus, I see you at the cross,
late in the grey-grief afternoon.
Women weeping—soldiers sleeping—disciples fleeing
and yet you came,
wrapped in a sorrowful cloak.
Together you helped
Joseph of Arimathea slip the body soundlessly
from the humbled tree—
stumbling under the precious weight—

to the garden, a green olive-sweet garden with a new tomb.

Nicodemus, I see you in the Duomo in Florence
on a Son-light morning, standing
under Bruneleschi's dome.
You . . . you immortalized by Michelangelo
sculpting his features in your marble face.

Palpable sorrow and eternal praise
chiseled together in the passionate Pieta,
polished centuries after the Tomb was empty.

John 3

MARY MAGDALENE ON EASTER MORNING

Early in the morning on the first day of the week, while it was still dark, Mary Magdalene came to the tomb and saw that the STONE was moved away from the entrance. She ran at once to Simon Peter and the other disciple, the one Jesus loved, breathlessly panting, They took the Master from the TOMB. We don't know where they have put Him.
John 20

We are told that as Mary stood weeping she looked again into the dark recesses to see the glowing light of two Angels, one sitting at the head and the other at the foot of the ledge where Jesus had lain. The Angels asked her:

Why are you weeping? She turned away and saw Jesus standing there, but she, thinking that he was the gardener asked: If you took him, tell me where you put him so I can care for him. Jesus said, Mary. Turning to look at him she said Rabboni! meaning Teacher. John 20

Jesus told her not to cling to Him for He had not yet ascended to His Father, but to go and give the incredible news to the disciples that He was alive! And so it was that a faithful woman, a woman who had been made whole by the Great Physician, was the very first to be commissioned to tell the world that Jesus was Living Water.

Come—move silently as stars
under the hood of night,
no time now for tears or fright.
Joanna, please hold Mary's arm
we must shield her from any more harm.

Mother of James, I cannot lift these bags alone,
this Frankincense and Myrrh weigh like stone.
Ladies, I know your hearts are heavy as sin . . .
life will move on—we must tell others of Him.

Listen—the rooster crows dawn,
make haste before the black robe is gone.
The morning comes quickly on Angel wings
in the sky, clouds flee—birds sing.
The Father signs His signature in red,
the color of blood on the Sacred Head.

Wait, who rolled the stone?
Men could not do that alone—
down—yes—but not up the hillside!

I dared not think how we'd get inside.
Now it stands open for all the world to see

but His body is not here—the Tomb is empty!

Go—go and tell—the Risen Lord commands!
Friends, let's clasp hands,
we must hurry and pray,

The disciples will listen when we say
He is Risen!

He is Risen indeed!

Amen

Luke 24

PETER AT THE TOMB

The fisherman was out of his own depth when he scrambled up the rough path and looked into the tomb of the One who had named him the Rock. The One who had revolutionized his life. The One who had shown him everything about himself, his strengths and weaknesses. On the stormy sea when he had found himself walking on the waves as if they were silk, he took his eyes off of Jesus and floundered, gasping for breath. And he cried:

Lord, save me! Jesus lifted him from the waves and said: O man of little faith, why did you doubt? Matthew 14

Rubbing red-rimmed eyes, Peter doubted yet again. The crowing cock still echoed in his ears. The linen cloth was there and the head-piece—His prayer shawl—the knotted fringe representing the laws of God was crusted now with His life-blood. The shawl was folded separately as a careful Jew would do. But the body of his Master, his Friend, and his Hope was missing!

John was fast, yes,
but I was not frightened.
I was first.

I bowed my head low,
ducked into the sanctified space.
I saw the exhausted grave clothes—
the bloody head-piece—folded—alone.

But why—why did I not see
the Angel messenger?

Was I too bound by earthly cares,
rooted in my own reasoning,
incapable of seeing Angel's wings?

My eyes were clouded these days of grief,
remembering the painful past—
unable to behold the promised future.
My spirit weighted like a net,
shrouded my heart from hope,
prevented me from sensing the Heavenly Presence.

The Angel spoke with Mary Magdalene
and the other women—golden
words of Resurrection and direction.

What did they see?
Why?
How?

Was her mind open to new possibility,
free to accept miraculous divinity,

eyes focused on radical reality?
Her spirit soaring with hope,
recognizing the Heavenly?

O, woe is me!

And what about John?
Why didn't he see?

The Gospels

DEAR DR. LUKE

Very early on a bright Easter morning when I was meditating on the Scripture that illumines faith and rereading the familiar pages, I imagined myself as a woman of the first century. Perhaps I lived inside the golden walls of Jerusalem, in a fine stone house.

Servants were preparing the feast for family and friends and I was free to contemplate my questions. I wrote this letter to the well-known Dr. Luke whom Paul had called the beloved physician. I had heard of the Doctor's writings to his friend Theophilus:

Several biographies of Christ have already been written using as their source material the reports circulating among us from the early disciples and other eye-witnesses. However, it occurred to me that it would be well to recheck all of these accounts from first to last and after thorough investigation to pass this summary on to you, to reassure you of the truth of all you were taught. Luke 1

Dear Dr. Luke:

Your writings interest me therefore I am writing to request a consultation in your office. Will I find it on the street of the Prophets? You write with great authority of what has already happened. I understand you traveled extensively with the Apostle Paul. Did you know him first as Saul? Can the medical profession affect such an amazing transformation of the spirit?

And what do you know of Jesus of Nazareth? Perhaps you were a wedding guest when wine was sweeter at the end than the beginning—is that within your alchemy? Or were you in Alexandria or Rome at your studies while these miracles exploded like shooting stars across our land? Did you witness the Resurrection or even a healing—has such lightning ever fired your fingertips? How could that woman who touched Him have bled for a dozen years—poured out her very life like rain on a dusty road?

O, I must apologize kind sir. I sound as if I am interviewing you. What I meant to do was set forth three questions that trouble me, for your consideration before we meet, if you will indeed do me the honor since I am but a humble woman. You will find my needs are more of the spirit than the body. I appreciate your fine reputation of treating the whole person not just the symptoms. Please indulge me my questions.

1. Where is the seat of faith—in the mind or in the heart?
2. Why is it that enthusiasm can spike like fever and

fall so quickly in the face of opposition?

3. How am I to deal with my desire, like a rising thunderhead, to be made new, transformed, by a process I do not understand?

My young nephew will wait for your reply. Please, good Dr. Luke, if you will be so kind to see me as an anxious patient needing your healing touch. For my malady is of the spirit if not the body.

Faithfully yours,

Alegria
14th of Nissan

Luke 1

NOW

MASSIVE EARTHQUAKE ROCKS 9.0 ON
THE 10 POINT RICHTER SCALE!

TECTONIC PLATE OF INDIAN OCEAN
FLOOR MOVES 98 FEET!

ISLANDS DISAPPEAR!

TSUNAMI WAVES COST 300,000 LIVES!

PLANET EARTH WOBBLES ON ITS AXIS!

DAYS PERMANENTLY SHORTENED
BY A FRACTION!

And we ask with Pilate. What is TRUTH?

And you shall know the Truth and the Truth shall set you free. John 8

Where is HOPE?

We who run for our very lives to God have every reason to grab the promised Hope with both hands and never let go. It's an unbreakable spiritual lifeline. Hebrews 6

And what of PEACE?

For he himself is our Peace. Ephesians 2

THOMAS EVERYMAN

You, Thomas, disciple of Jesus, asked the questions that so many people need answered. And you had been with Him three years, walked, talked, ate, and witnessed His miracles. With a knowing smile He gave you a basket of leftover bread and fish on that mountainside. You were there when the lame walked and the blind saw. And yet—yet—belief came hard, like sleeping on the rocky ground and not feeling rested.

I won't believe it unless I see the nail wounds in his hands— and put my fingers into them—and place my hand into his side. Eight days later the Disciples were together again and this time Thomas was with them. The doors were locked; but suddenly as before, Jesus was standing among them and greeting them. Then he said to Thomas: put your finger into my hands. Put your hand into my side. Don't be faithless any longer. Believe! Thomas said: My Lord and my God! John 20

NOW you knew that everything had changed.

Thomas, you must be cousin to everyone.
So many claim to be like you,
full as sunrise of doubt and fear,
uncertain what the day may bring.
When night falls they hide their heads
under pillows of piety, blankets of blindness,
claiming they will not believe unless they see.
Poor relations, these, to charge
their doubts to your overdrawn account.

For you Thomas had followed Him
some three years through storms and starlight.
Why? Why were you not with the Brothers
in fellowship when He came?
Doubt? Dread? Discouragement?
Even for Disciples? Yes
we too know these demons well.

You were not chided by the Lord
for questions, but for absence.

You missed rejoicing with friends
when He appeared fresh from the Tomb!
You missed His blessing of the Passover Peace!
You missed the Dedication Commissioning
when Jesus breathed His Holy Spirit power into them!

Eight days later you brought your questions
inside the locked door. Questions
do not negate faith, rather,
answered questions validate trust.
Trust—is the first and final step of faith.

In loving kindness Jesus appeared again,
extended scarred hands directly to you.
Falling at His pierced feet—you knew the answer
to all questions—

My Lord and My God!

John 20

THE BLIND MAN

We are all born blind. As infants we are blind to our Spiritual potential. As our eyes of understanding are opened we long for clear sight. Vision is all too often clouded by tragic realities. And we cannot dream of the future when we are imprisoned in the NOW. All too often we are stuck in the present and cannot see beyond right NOW. But when we meet the Light of Life, His brilliance transcends all darkness and we dare to hope of what could be true when we walk with Him.

Jesus asked the blind man named Bartimaeus:

What do you want me to do for you? Rabbi, I want to see. On your way, said Jesus. Your faith has saved and healed you. Mark 10

But what of me if I have no faith to tap into the power of the One who designed eyes and I am groping in the dark? When Jesus encountered another blind man He gave him a specific action:

He spit in the dust, made a clay paste with the saliva rubbed the paste on the blind man's eyes, and said, "Go; wash in the pool of Siloam." The man went and washed and saw. John 9

He healed not only that blind man but gave an object lesson to the bystanders who had been listening to His claims of Divinity. For they knew the spittle of the eldest son was considered to be miraculous, but not like this! Could He truly be the Son of God?

What is blue?
You tell me the sky is a bowl of blue,
a bowl I know—but blue?
No light penetrates these chasms of darkness
only bitter blue questions—
why was I born blind?

What is yellow?
You tell me the sun is a yellow ball,
a ball I know—but yellow?
No hope brightens these pools of blackness,
only yellow yearning for all I cannot see.

What is red?
You tell me the fire is red, blazing wood,
wood I know—but red?
Only red rage burns these useless sockets,
that I must beg, not work as others labor.

What is orange?
You tell me an orange is orange.

An orange I know—but orange?
Do not mock me—or the sweet
juice on my beard turns sour in my mouth.

But thank God I hear—hear
the hawking cries of peddlers, babies crying,
crowds whispering—whispering Who is He?
A shadow of coolness crosses my face, a tender
touch presses damp clay to these empty holes.
I stumble to the pool of Siloam—Sabbath worshippers
passing me by—stumble again, falling on my face—
washing as I was told. White light
splashes through clouds of doubt
and joy moves in new eyes like Spirit wind.

What is green?
You tell me grass is green, grass I know,
but green must be grace—green-grace to see.
Now I see grass, trees, leaves are green—
green-grace for growing things.

What is violet?
You tell me violet is the last of the rainbow,
the rainbow I know, for through my tears
I see red orange yellow green blue violet vision
for once I was blind and now—now I see.

John 9

THE LAD WITH TWO FISH

NOW it had been at least three years since he had met Jesus on that hillside. He understood everything, really everything had changed. Momentous events had occurred in Jerusalem and the news of it was spreading rapidly across the Galilee like a fresh wind. He remembered like it was yesterday.

It was just a little lunch. He had stood on a rock at the water's edge, eying intently the quick fish darting in and out of the cool blue shadows. The sun was climbing higher, soon he must be on his way, fish or no fish. His mother only had a few small rolls to give him this morning; there were many mouths to feed from her meager supply. Maybe the fishermen had it easier than the farmer who had to work the ground, plant the seed, pray for rain and wait and wait and wait. It seemed all of life was consumed with waiting, and just getting enough to eat.

Was there ever to be more meaning to his life than waiting? Was anyone out there listening to the rambling thoughts of a young boy? What did it all mean? Did life have any kind of a greater purpose? He waited and wondered . . .

Look at the birds, they don't worry about what to eat—
they don't need to sow or reap or store up food—for
your Heavenly Father feeds them. And you are far more

valuable to him than they are. Your Heavenly Father
already knows perfectly well what you need and he will
give them to you if you give him first place in your life
and live as he wants you to. Matthew 6

The loaves were still warm this morning
when you tied them in a ragged blue cloth,
bread crusty as sun-baked bricks—inside
soft as your mother's kiss.
The jig line was slow to net two fish—
barely enough to feed a cat.
You had an errand for a sick friend in Capernaum,
the sun already hot
and you'd best be back by nightfall . . .

The Man was speaking from a fishing boat
at the shore of the blue-green sea.
A large crowd was gathered on the hillside—
the grass looked cool and green as olives.

More people were listening to Him
than even lived in your village!
What could be so important?

Finding a small rock under a tree
you sat down—wishing

those white blossoms were sweet oranges right now.

The Man speaking—His strong voice
rolling around the cup-shaped hill—
said you were blessed if you were poor,
that you would be comforted if you were sad,
that it was good to be a peacemaker.

Like when your Papa got angry with Mama?

You stomach growled like a hungry
lion but no one was eating.

One man was asking questions—he laughed
when you offered to give your lunch to the Man
who said such surprising things—he laughed,
but he took it to Jesus.

That was His name you found out later—
Jesus thanked His Father in Heaven for your little lunch,
then He broke off pieces for everybody—
you had five whole fish yourself!
He even had twelve baskets left over—
one basket for each of His helpers!

Years later perhaps you learned to
write Aramaic and Hebrew
with the patience honed of jig lines and errands.

Maybe Matthew hired you to copy carefully
those wonderful words
on the precious leather scrolls—

Blessed are the Peacemakers.

Matthew 5

MATTHIAS

Matthias, your real life began after the Resurrection of the Messiah. Church history identifies you as one of the 70 whom Jesus had previously sent out *"two by two into every town and place where he was about to come."* But when you were chosen by lot to be the new 12th apostle it was because you had been with Jesus from his baptism all the way down the dusty roads to the mountain of His Ascension. And tradition records that you preached the Good News in Judea until you also were martyred for the faith.

The story is told of a missionary arriving home into New York Harbor after twenty-five years on the foreign field. As his eyes scanned the boisterous crowd he could find no one who was there to welcome him. No representative of the mission board he had so faithfully served. No old friends, no one from his church, no one at all. O, he had been home on furlough a few times—the usual round of chicken dinners, polite questions, captive audiences for his pictures, but little time for real sharing from the heart. He felt like a displaced person. And then that still small voice that always whispered deep in his soul reminded him that he was not home yet.

The good ground represents the heart of the man who listens to the message and understands it and goes

*out and brings thirty, sixty or even a hundred others into
the Kingdom. Matthew 13*

Matthias!
Unsung hero—invisible man—
forgotten servant, what was your name again?

Matthias!
A record empty as wind down a deserted road,
no paper trail, no reference of service.
Did you pray—teach—heal—or write?
Were you on the hillside for the miraculous picnic,
or in the funeral procession at Nain?
Were you in the Synagogue at Capernaum,
where did you first see Him?

The last time was on the Mountaintop as the Cloud
gathered Him into the white silence—
the wind as empty as your heart
on that sorrowful Sabbath day journey.

You knew the baptism of John in the
holy name of the Father
and the Son, were numbered among
the 120 followers of Messiah,

drawn together like clouds before a storm.

Matthias!
The thunder of your name in that upper room
startled you like jangling coins spilled on the stones.

Matthias!
The lot fell to you to fill the shamed office of Judas.
You fell to your knees—
unsung hero of the faith—
invisible man of the Scripture—
forgotten servant of Jesus.

The wind-wrapped fire of the Holy Spirit
seared your mind,
baptized your soul,
filled your heart.

Matthias!
The first of all
unsung,
invisible,
forgotten
Missionaries.

Acts 1

BARNABAS

If you carry a sack of stones it gets heavy before you travel very far. At first it is just a few stones that you pick up along the way. Then your fingers begin to cramp, arm muscles strain, shoulders tense and your back hurts.

A pebble of disappointment,
     another of doubt,
a stone of disease,
     another of disillusionment,
a rock of discouragement,
     another of despair,
a boulder of disaster
     another of disbelief,
until finally you have reached a mountain
     named desperation.

That is when you need to meet an encourager like Barnabas. He came from Cyprus where he had sold his property to give support to the messengers of the Good News about Resurrection Life. He traveled with Paul and served the ever-growing community of faith. He fulfilled the meaning of his name, son of encouragement.

Barnabas, where was the property that you sold,
on the wind or leeward side of the almond-shaped island
of Cyprus? And your livelihood—
fisherman, farmer or merchant?
O, to sit across a little beach table
from you, feet in the sand,
shaded by a white umbrella, listening to
the music of the Mediterranean,
eating fish that swam but an hour ago,
and salt you with questions, Barnabas the encourager.

Was the wind strong the first day that you boarded a ship
in Paphos for the journey of several days, to Joppa
in the beautiful land and on up the hills until
you reached the high wall of Jerusalem?

Entering her Joppa gate the cacophony of sounds
must have assaulted ears tuned to the whistle of sea gulls;
peddlers with push carts hawking their wares, wheels
clattering over cobblestones, the braying of animals,
iron clanging iron in the blacksmith's shop, coins
ringing in a ceramic dish and the confusion of languages.
Children playing hide and seek
in the labyrinth of shops and narrow alleyways.

Ripe smells—new to a nose trained to salt air—
oranges in the sun, coffee roasting in small copper pans,
big baskets of figs and dates oozing juice,
bread carried on the boy's head, women hurrying

to put their pots of meat and vegetables
in the glowing coals of the baker's oven.

Passover time in Jerusalem.
You must have prayed with the Disciples,
debated long hours into the night the implications
of Messiah's commands. It was a significant sacrifice
to sell your quiet land at home and give the money
for missions. Little did you dream that soon
you, Barnabus of Cyprus, and Paul of Tarsus,
a city far to the north, would sit at a little beach table,
feet in the sand of Paphos, shaded by a white umbrella,
listening to the music of the Mediterranean
and eat fish that swam but an hour ago,
all because the Master said
"Go."

Acts 4

ETERNITY

ADAM FELL HARD AGAINST THE
LODESTONE OF GOD'S COMMANDS

ABRAHAM USED HIS SHARPENING STONE DAILY

JACOB DREAMT ON A PILLOW
OF STONE AT BETHEL

MOSES CAME DOWN FROM MT. SINAI
WITH TWO TABLETS OF STONE

JOSHUA RAISED ALTARS OF
JORDAN RIVER STONES

DAVID CHOSE FIVE SMOOTH
STONES TO FELL GOLIATH

SOLOMON ORDERED TEMPLE STONES
HEWN FROM HIS QUARRY

DANIEL SAW A STONE FROM THE
MOUNTAIN CRUSH THE IMAGE

JOHN THE BAPTIST STOOD ON
A PULPIT OF STONE

PAUL PREACHED ABOUT THE
STONE IDOLS OF ATHENS

PETER CALLED BELIEVERS LIVING STONES

JESUS WAS CALLED A STONE OF
STUMBLING TO THE FAITHLESS

JESUS WAS CALLED THE CORNERSTONE,
AND THE CAPSTONE

God has used ordinary stones and ordinary people of His creation to build up the great truths of the Scripture on the unshakeable foundation of the Lord Jesus Christ.
John the Apostle writes near the end of his life:

I have written this to you who believe so that you may know that you have ETERNAL LIFE.
1John 5

THE APOSTLE JOHN ON PATMOS

John, son of Zebeedee, you were one of the first to follow the young man from Nazareth. You walked and talked and ate with Him, saw almost all of the miracles, became His closest friend. At the cross, He in agony thought of His Mother, Mary, and asked you to care for her.

Tradition suggests that the two of you traveled as far as Ephesus where you continued to tell and record the remarkable stories of His life and love. You also were encouragers because you had known Jesus more closely than any of the others had. You had observed the truth of His life, the consistency of His words and the impeccable purity of His character. You were able to write with absolute authority about the transforming power of His Resurrected Life when it is linked by faith to the believing life of any man, woman or child.

Fearful that the whole world might follow the Christ caused Domitian, the Emperor of Rome, to reach out to imprison you on the Isle of Patmos, isolated in the blue Aegean Sea. But he could not have imagined how your written words—words of unprecedented visions—would be circulated to give hope to men and women everywhere in the Revelation of Jesus Christ.

And I heard a loud shout from the Throne saying,
Look, the home of God is now among men, and he

will live with them and they will be his people;
yes, God himself will be among them. He will wipe
away all tears from their eyes, and there shall be no
death, nor sorrow, nor crying, nor pain. Revelation 21

The cave was cold.
COLD as the Emperor Domitian's steel sword,
you, banished to that rocky heap in the goat sea,
a nonagenarian, having cared for Mary and
spoken good news to the citizens of Ephesus.

The food was scarce.
SCARCE as berries on a wind-thrashed bush.
No monastery yet founded on the precarious peak where
you could have savored steaming soup with a saint
or two, ruminating over the remarkable 1st century;
remembering the blessings of fish in nets, heavy,
almost tearing your arms; and that final
breakfast on the beach.

The ground was hard.
HARD as sorrow for bonded brothers, all martyred
by sword, arrows, hurled knives, saws,
poison, hanging or upside down crucifixion.
When blackness shrouded the sun, you wrapped
yourself in grief and prayer and slept.

The stars were exploding.
EXPLODING into angels, horses, rainbows, earthquakes,
jewels, fire, seals, and golden bowls,
all to the fanfare of majestic trumpets.
At first light, gathering your robe around old bones—after
lying prostrate in reverent awe—you
took your precious pen,
beginning to record the wondrous vision as commanded
by the voice of the Resurrected Life.

The fire was scorching.
SCORCHING your soul, burning words
appeared on the papyrus, infused
in the fibers by the Spirit, Himself,
exactly as you had seen it—terrible—
glorious beyond all imagining.

The Celestial City was opening.
OPENING pearl gates in jeweled walls to
golden streets beside the crystal sea.
The living hand of the Great Physician
dried your tears as you faithfully addressed
the timeless letters to Ephesus, Smyrna
Pergamum, Thyatira, Sardis, Philadelphia, Laodicea.

Revelation 1

ISAIAH AND THE DINNER GUEST

Heaven will be full of wonderful surprises! One of the current popular books suggests whom you will meet in Heaven. Did you ever wonder whom you will know for all of ETERNITY? Whom will you look for beyond family? Some will surprise you, whom you wrongly judged, others will be strangely missing—all talk, but no real heart for God. But have you ever considered the wonder of the centuries collapsing like a landslide of rocks and rubble and everyone finding himself together on level ground at the foot of the cross?

The prophets were not popular in their day—their messages from God were often difficult warnings of severe judgment for the unrepentant. But these timeless books are also brimming with hope and comfort for all ETERNITY.

The Apostle Paul admonishes Timothy that:

Every part of Scripture is God-breathed and useful one way or another—showing us truth, exposing our rebellion, correcting our mistakes, training us to live God's way. Through the Word we are put together and shaped up for the tasks God has for us. II Timothy 3:15

When the prophet Isaiah lived, seven hundred years before Christ, he wrote many of the most remarkable prophecies, truths he could not possibly have known by himself. These included not only the sign that the baby would miraculously be born of a virgin, but also the future names by which He would be known.

For unto us a child is born, unto to us a Son is given and the government shall be upon his shoulder: and his name shall be called Wonderful, Counselor, The Mighty God, The Everlasting Father, The Prince of Peace. Isaiah 9

Centuries later these very names
resonated with Fredrick Handel.

Reservations for Dinner at eight—
Martha's Bethany Inn, a table for two in a quiet corner
not a romantic tryst but a meeting of kindred spirits.
An extraordinary partnership which never met on earth,
The Prophet Isaiah and Fredrick Handel,
Heaven's finest librettist and composer, a team
like Rodgers and Hammerstein or Gaither and Lowry,
meeting for the first time over dinner and wine.

For you had not shared the same century—
one seven hundred years before the year of Our Lord,
the other seventeen centuries after His death.
Yet you had a melodious meeting of the minds.

Fredrick Handel, you must have arrived early at Martha's
out of respect, you were much the
younger to the venerable
Prophet Isaiah, son of Amoz, servant
to four Kings of Judah.
Did you ever travel to Jerusalem
from your home in London,
or simply imagine in sacred meditation
the Mountain on which Messiah will stand?
When did Isaiah's glorious words grip you with awe?
At what age did you hear music to that which Isaiah saw?
You never spoke in person, yet made Isaiah's
immortal truth your very own.

Isaiah, I think you and Handel lingered long over coffee.
Questions sparkled in the candlelight.
How did you know that a Virgin would bear a Son,
or even that His name was to be Immanuel?
And all of His Royal names, Wonderful, Counselor,
The Mighty God, The Everlasting
Father, The Prince of Peace.

Thank you, Gentlemen.
Heaven's Halls will ring with your Oratorio,
"And He shall reign for ever and ever."
King of Kings and Lord of Lords

Isaiah 7

MICAH THE PROPHET

The citizens of earth will *drink the wine of astonishment (Psalm 60)* when they finally connect the dots that you have spaced out in your prophecy. Like a child's party game it will be so easy to see the pictures outlined, filled in, and colored perfectly. Readers will puzzle over having missed the message before. Of course if we do not read the instruction manual for life—the Bible—we simply draw our own conclusions and decide that life is a game of multi-colored choices. Like balloons at a birthday party—some will explode right in our foolish faces.

He has told you, O man, what is good; and what does the Lord require of you but to do justice, to love kindness, and to walk humbly with your God? Micah 6

Micah, how did you know
those long crenellated centuries ago?
Was your wisdom written with the ink of age
that we should read your words on a printed page?
Was your visionary insight revealed on bomb-bright nights
that the United Nations should quote
you, but continue to fight?
Was your discernment so supernaturally understood

that you knew what the Lord requires to do good?

Micah, you served three kings of
Judah as a prophet of God.
Good Kings who heeded advice to walk humbly with God;
Jotham, Ahaz, and Hezekiah reigned
61 years, loving justice—
the measure of men who serve the
Lord of mercy and justice.
Men still look for the day when every king and nation
will beat their swords to plowshares
and be brother relations.

Micah, how did you know,
those long crenellated centuries ago
that the Prince of Peace would be born in Bethlehem,
even Bethlehem-Ephratah in the south, not the north land?
Micah, true wordsmith, though your writings are small
you revealed God's eternal Truth for all
men and nations to make war no more.

On that opening New York night
the United Nations will bow before
The King of Kings and Lord of Lords.

Micah 4

POLITICALLY CORRECT

Leah Rabin in memory of her husband, Yitzhak Rabin

The Heroes of any conflict are those who lay down their lives in order that their countrymen may live in peace and safety. This has been the elusive goal of the Middle East for centuries, particularly since May 1948 when statehood for Israel was proclaimed. In these Biblical lands the anger boils in a black cauldron on a fire of thorns, and frequently spills over on anyone who is in the way. So many leaders in the way of peace have been victims of their own bravery.

One such leader was Yitzhak Rabin, former Prime Minister of Israel. He was assassinated as he was speaking to a crowd in a public square about hope for peace. Soon afterward his grieving widow was interviewed by a ruthless reporter, gunning for a hot story.

The relentless reporter frowned,
"What do you remember most?"
expecting an answer politically correct.
"It was the way he lay on the ground."

Crowds were pressing all around,
fractured air—frozen time—silent screams—

a rushing river of grief babbling
over the way he lay on the ground.

Sirens wailed their mourning sound.
Another leader fallen in fighting for peace.
The assassin sneered
at the way he lay on the ground.

Husband—daddy—grandfather—down,
all the world hushed to hear,
Mrs. Rabin stoically repeat,
"It was the way he lay on the ground."

THE WAY IT COULD BE

On a warm afternoon in Jerusalem still another staccato burst of gunfire erupted on a narrow street in a quiet neighborhood. Keening cries swept the stone canyons as seven girls lay in their own seeping blood, grotesque patterns of war freshly painted on the thirsty stones. They were victims of the Intifada—victims whose only crime was being Jewish.

Suddenly an extraordinary event crackled the news lines as word of Jordan's King Hussein coming to Jerusalem spread like grass fire. He spent that awful afternoon in the homes of the seven girls who had been slain. Going from house to house he sat with the stunned parents, grieving over pictures of the dead, listening to the hopes and dreams now vanished in the acrid smoke hanging in the breathless air.

Shots shattered the Shabbat afternoon,
seven daughters of Zion slumped down,
never to live or love again.
Weeping poured out all over town.

Anger fired the following days.
Seven families mourned, kneeling down,

never to see their girls grow up,
weeping poured out all over the town.

Compassion moved the Jordanian King,
visiting the families, he knelt down,
shared stories, pictures of their slain pride,
weeping poured for the divided town.

"This is the way it could be, "
an observant reporter wrote down,
if brothers lived in unity,
weeping for joy would change this town.

Soon after, the funeral cortege of this same King
brought world leaders to his Amman-town
to honor a man of great compassion.
Weeping poured out in both towns.

In memory of King Hussein of Jordan

ANGEL OF HOPE

Angels are all around us—on pins and key rings, candles and greeting cards. Do we believe that those things represent anything in the real world? Or is it just wishful thinking that we each have a guardian angel, when in reality their wings would melt just like candle wax? The Bible records hosts—tens of thousands—of angels who are a created order of heavenly beings.

You have made man only a little lower than the angels, and placed a crown of glory and honor on his head.
Psalm 8

Three Angels are named: rebellious Lucifer; Michael, the defender of Israel; and the glorious messenger, Gabriel, who appeared to Mary the virgin, Joseph, and Zacharias. Angels spoke with many other people like Abraham, Sarah, Lot, Jacob, Manoah and his wife, and Paul and Silas. These Angelic messengers of God are all around us, listening for instructions to answer God's call.

Are you the Resurrection Angel from the Tomb?
Are you Gabriel the Good News messenger or
Michael, the protector of Israel who

declared victorious Messiah
will stand on Mt. Olivet again on that
glorious cloudless morning?

Or are you the Angel who
opened Hagar's eyes to see the well,
visited Abraham and made Sarah laugh,
took Lot's wife's hand to lead her to safety,
or stood on Jacob's ladder, or wrestled and lamed his hip,
flew death-wings over Egypt seeking blood-marked doors,
or directed Moses and Elijah to the
same, safe cave on Mt. Horeb?

Are you perhaps the Angel who scared
the poor donkey into speaking
or visited Samson's parents for a sacred vow,
met David at the threshing floor of Aranuah
or encamps around the people of God
walked in fire and shut the lion's mouth
or stood astride the River Euphrates to speak with Daniel
touched Isaiah's lips with live coals from the altar
or talked with Zechariah about the apple of the Lord's eye?

Did you, strong Angel, shake away Peter's chains
and unlock prison doors,
or are you an Angel of the seven churches,
perhaps lukewarm Ladodica or loving Philadelphia?

Are you in the Bethlehem Chorale:
Seraphim, Cherubim, Guardian, or Warrior?
Do you attend the Mercy Seat
or carry prayers on waves of incense sweet,
and tell me do you mark your place around the Throne
when far from home?

Whatever your name or fame,
I call you Angel of Hope.
When you sound the *Shofar*,
rending Heaven's star-strung veil,

Every eye shall see Him,

The Resurrected One,
Messiah in King's robes
descending the rainbow galaxy.
His scarred feet will split The Mount of Olives
from east to west—refuge for the remnant.
Armageddon will cease
before the scepter of the Prince of Peace.

Hallelujah,
Hallelujah,
Hallelujah

Acts I

RESURRECTION LIFE

Do you ever ask yourself, "What is Resurrection Life?" Is it only the pale morning of hope in the distant future when I might come back to life after the dust of death? Is it the exquisite promise of life eternal that people of faith talk of in ethereal whispers? Is it just an adult fairy tale or a panacea of peace talk to get us through dreary days and dream-racked nights?

Jesus Christ, the only Resurrected Life, claimed:

I have come that you might have life and have it more abundantly. John 10

Not just wonderful hope and peace for the future, but life at its best now. He was speaking of the quality of life available to those who would follow Him as the Good Shepherd all the way home.

The characteristics of that kind of life include:

Love, joy, peace, patience, kindness, goodness, faithfulness, gentleness, and self-control. Galatians 5

The mountains will seem impossible but He knows where the mountain pass lies. The way will undoubtedly be rocky; sometimes stones big and small will mark the route. But through it all I have found that it is possible in the Resurrection Life today to exchange:

> fear for faith
> horror for hope
> lust for love
> confusion for confidence.

Therefore if any man be in Christ, he is a new creature; the old things have passed away, behold, new things have come. 11 Corinthians 5

I pray His peace and promises will give you daily joy for the journey.

THE MARBLE PROMISE

Let not your heart be troubled: you believe in God, believe also in me. In my Father's house are many mansions: if it were not so, I would have told you. I go to prepare a place for you. And if I go and prepare a place for you, I will come again and receive you unto myself; that where I am, there you may be also. John 14

Miracles of Resurrection Life surround us at all times, from the first promised blush of morning to the Daystar after the darkest night. Every day citizens of Heaven are welcomed home and new babies cry at the first gulp of air. Every breath we take, heartbeat, step, every good idea and imaginative plan is due to the Resurrection Life. Every blade of grass, opening crocus, budded tree, rain drop, snowflake, lady bug and butterfly is because He lives. Every healing and recovery, every drink of water, every grain of rice is from the touch of His nail-scarred hand. All faith, all hope, all truth is found in the one Resurrected Life.

I am the Resurrection and the Life, he who believes in me shall live even if he dies, and everyone who lives and believes in me shall never die. John 11

The marble tombs of Kings
weigh heavy on the earth,
freighted folds of satin and velvet
shroud familiar forms.
Jeweled crowns chiseled on smooth brows,
sightless eyes in peaceful repose,
beautiful hands unstenciled by life.
Belts and buckles and fur, so cold,
wrapped against the cathedral night.
Polished boots that never did battle,
did they stand so tall in deeds?

Where is the tomb of the
King of the Jews?
Why no Michelangelo commission
to chose the choicest Carrara
for a final masterpiece?
Why no funds for new-forged tools
unmarred by chipping bones of stone?
Why no studio provided, swept clean
of the Pieta's tears?
Why, please tell me why?
Is earth too fragile for another marble tomb?

The marble master could have carved
again that thorn-crushed brow,
eyes pressed in pain,
scarred hands mapped with healing.
The broken body, cross-twisted

without royal robes
or boots for bloodied feet.
Why, please tell me why,
is the world sinking under monuments?

No marble bower could hold mercy's weight,
no cathedral could contain His grace,
no tomb could hold His love.
He is not here, He is risen, the angel said,
and as He promised, one day soon,
The King of Kings will break through
the marble dome of heaven.

Revelation 22

ABOUT THE AUTHOR

Joyce Carr Stedelbauer is an accomplished poet, author, and a highly sought speaker. Her previous book, *Have You Seen the Star?*, was chosen for the Midwest Book Review Selection Award. In addition to serving as a deacon at the Williamsburg Community Chapel, she teaches two Bible studies weekly. Joyce is an active member of the International Sisters-in-Service, National League of American Pen Women, The Poetry Society of Virginia, and The Williamsburg Poetry Guild. She and her husband, George, have a son and daughter, both of them graduates of Wheaton College, and five grandchildren. Their home is in Williamsburg but they are often traveling the world, always with the desire to encourage other believers and point people to Christ.

Contact Joyce Carr Stedelbauer
or order more copies of this book at

TATE PUBLISHING, LLC

127 East Trade Center Terrace
Mustang, Oklahoma 73064

(888) 361 - 9473

Tate Publishing, LLC

www.tatepublishing.com